Praise for (

It's kind of irresistible, Chris's poems have a page turner thing, very daily, very noir and yet there's this sweet sense of awe — that "this" is happening to me and that I have a life is ultimately good news for all of us — this sensation of his is really one long poem.

—Eileen Myles

The clippings of these poems' toenails are already all over your bedsheets, so why the hell not get some beauty for your trouble? And the beauty of (laughter) is potent magic. This book will sit with you on the curb your heavy heart won't let you leave until the sun comes up and loan you its last four dollars. Test your own heart's dilapidated walls with some poems that know you better than you know yourself.

—Geoff Munsterman, author of
Because the Stars Shine Through It (Lavender Ink)

(laughter)

Christopher Heffernan

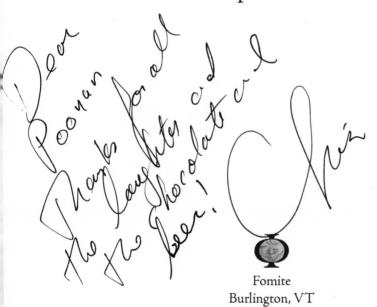

Fomite
Burlington, VT

ISBN-13: 978-1-959984-20-7
Library of Congress Control Number: 2023942642

Fomite
58 Peru Street
Burlington, VT 05401
www.fomitepress.com

08-17-2023

Contents

(laughter)

A Filthy Way

it is a filthy
way

my hands

are in
           my pockets

still cut
           with scabs

and lines
of blood streaked
and turned like streets

on a map of where

I went

beyond

(far beyond)

all those pretty
  words
           I use

the ones
that so many others

seem to understand
so   much
                better

In The Place Of We

this
fixed
one

full

in
the
ribs
of having
had

ripped

the
flame

up
from
the
breath

outside

our
moon
light
beauty

with
a
blue
hand

holding
a
rope

for
what
is
one
step

beyond

the
how
it
is
happening

no
matter
what
you
say

no
matter
how
it tears
at
you

to build
always
with
confetti

type
tatters
from
what's
been
left
behind

this
thing
that
some
will
call
love

Of This Way

you push

many times

when you
shouldn't push

and hope
when you
shouldn't hope

hoping sometimes
for things you
don't even want

and

it is obvious
looking out

from under
your eyes

what has been lost

in this space
without noise

on the earth

(the only place
we know)

(that dances death and miracles)

then

the lit end
of a cigarette

and with a slight
look to the side
you see

a difference
and distance

and the luster
is
small

but
when you grab
it

it burns your thumb
and finger
like the sun

a lightening
of pain

and a smell
that won't stop

as you wonder
while shaking
your hand for relief

if it will be back

going in

and going out

as
white ocean waves

knowing now
not to squeeze
your wound
so hard

and that the cherry glow
isn't a way
forward

but illuminates a
way forward

pointing

dimly
at times

toward

what
in the dark

refuses to close

Evening With You With Me

in
the open
street

lit
yellow
windows
and

this white
sidewalk

cement

with

what I see
        again

what I am
        told

walking
from
your
left
face looking
left
        now

from the side

that won't

answer
me

of a curb
cut

names

written in
broken glass

(the ways) I
      must hide

(with a hand on
      my brow)

from your
unblinking light knifey
     face

from
your pink shut up
      lips

Dog Egg

on the side
of a tin
pan

this city
falls out

of what is
to come

of fine curves
on four legs

barking
all the way

to where
the heat
goes numb

the dog egg
boils

in our
bitch
thoughts
heart

(always)

waiting
to be
received

Gross Faces

the last
time you
used your
hands to
make gross
faces

in the
hour

of
lying on
your back
and
watching
what was
supposed
to be
watching
you

waiting for a flinch

from either
side
of
the
fence

when kids
end what
kids' game ends

you write
your name
in your cheek
with a nail

(making
sure it's
still you)

                knowing
                there are
                so many
                choices
                today

another red
place

with the
heat of
the sun

and how
you understand

the waves
of what

hits the shore

(with no sound)

then
begging
you
to

follow

to be a
part of
the act

the way
you look
at me when
you say
perhaps
it will be
something
better

and for the
second time
tonight I
do not have
the heart
to tell you
the truth

There Is Secret Shit

there is secret shit
a secret smell to
secret meal
that is sometimes cake
sometimes water
wanting to eat want
with secret screams
that come as gray
hair in the eyes of
the old voice calling all
from the end of
what catches
light to turn red secret
roses red
from
secret dirt
driving
so still
an open space
seen only from
the earth looking up
a white
crater
smashed again
with the holes of
our hours
trying
to fill them warm
with what starts so raw

Space Girl

space girl was telling me how
she stole peanut butter from the
super market. they had this
machine that ground up fresh
peanuts and poured it right out
there for you and she'd make
herself a big container of it
then walk around the store
pretending to buy things as she
ate it all. then she would go back
and make a little more. just a
little and go up to the counter
and pay for that. "I feel bad,"
she would say, "I feel bad for
eating it all," she would say, "so
I buy a little." "Don't," I said,
"don't buy any," I said, "They're killing
us," I said, "We're all being killed,"
I said, "You gotta get something back,"
I said, "You gotta get something out
of this," I said. we weren't in love
or anything—just sitting on the curb
in front of Mimi's and she was telling
me about shopping and stealing
but then I was wondering what kissing her
would be like and sort of understood, looking
at her paint splattered pants and
filthy hands that it would be something
like kissing the craft table in a kindergarten—yes there
would be peanut butter, but also probably
the taste of paste and crayons

A Few Things

the other thing
I didn't do

the job

I always think
all the mosquitoes
have malaria and that
it's amazing anyone
survived the nineteenth
century

my neighbor's
dog eats cockroaches

three guys across the street
at the counter
stare into the street

wanting nothing
can be difficult, too

lying on the floor
throwing a tennis ball
into the air

the fictions of
some of the people
I know

(they go too far)

lay beyond a silly

interpretation

none of them
having ever forgotten
to sleep

apparently it can be
managed

apparently anything
can be managed

in the balance of
anger and not caring

in giving up
then getting up to
do it again

you find all the
different sounds
that laughter makes

that don't mean
laughter

that sometimes
mean the peace
of spilled blood

that sometimes are
the voices of
people telling you
to grieve more
for what is lost

pens, people, keys, people, etc

but you know
better

the tennis ball
knows better

it knows so well
how to exactly
come down the
way a tennis ball
comes down

your boss (my) boss

always thinking that if
he just had five more
minutes and ten more
dollars everything
would be alright

the way his eyes
move as he stumbles
from one moment
to the next

tangled up in
all that wasted
time

the friends I have known
quit from my life

(some from the Earth)

their five minutes
and their ten dollars

the cockroach-eating-dog
barks

yes, yes, the afternoon
has a sun

but this must be
managed, too

I imagine the look
on my face the
moment I have it
in my hand

the moment it
crushes my hand

at least I do not
lie to myself
that this is somehow
control

and then it is
gone

broken fingers
more laughter

like this

around
me

that which is
unpaved

and
enormous

mixed
in with

what the memories
of the dead I
continue to know

(they still have names)

keep
trying to tell
me

And It Won't Stop

the   truest   things

all   start   and

end   with   this

wanting

so badly

we've invented prayer
for it

and the

lottery

grabbing away
wildly

shoving
drooling
shitting
and puking

they are all there with
teeth and tits

knives guns and coffee

at home
in the schools
on the corner

throttling the last
bits of laughter
out of a clown
everyone hated
to begin with

no wonder no one
will

ride the bus anymore

Would

9:30

two quarters
a nickel

the lines on
the pavement
outside
the gas station

the
head
of the
man
behind
the
counter

my cracked lips

9:35

if i
smoked
cigarettes
anymore
i'd smoke
a cigarette
and give

the air
some
meaning

the street
going
      on
to
the
end
of   the
         city

through
the
small
circle
of each
streetlight

down the row

a
long
dark
dotted
hall

where
your
heart
goes

in your
ears

no
matter
how
much
you
beg
it
to

stop

no
matter
how
much
you
tell
what's
left
of
your
mind
to
please
stop
asking
questions

if
what
will
give

(give)

would
give

9:36

I'm Not Sure What This Means

from the hours

1) we fell off our
        toy   ponies

2) there had been some
        grinning and   singing

3) there was a baby
      giving directions
      (its head was talkyling smileyling)

4) go back five miles

5) turn slightly around

6) woke up at the kitchen
                   table

  had to figure out where
              I   was

7) sticking to the floor

8) it all looked so easy
      when   the others
          did   it

9) nothing else seems to
      be   coming
              now

She Was

she was
sitting on
the bus stop
bench in
handcuffs

the cop
about fifteen
feet away
talking on
what looked
like his phone

not a cb
or some
kind of
official
device

but a
regular
phone

pacing
around
by himself

we got
close enough
to her
to talk

but not

so close
to disturb
the cop
and his
phone call

her hands
were cuffed
in front of
her and
her hair was
a mess in
her face

and
she told
us what
happened
even though
we all knew
what happened

the cop kept
making circles
and was soon
so far
away
she could've got
up and run

but everyone
knew she
wasn't going
anywhere

because she knew

better than all of
us she wasn't
going anywhere

and then as
we said
goodbye and
started to leave

she said
out of nowhere,
you know,

(saying it to
the street and
not really to anyone
just the street
and the bench
and her bare feet)
you know
you can only
tear someone up
for so long
before you're
bored

and we stood
there not knowing
what to do
because

none of us
really had
anywhere
to be either

and
yeah
I guess
we all did
know that

and then the
cop hung up
his phone

and then immediately
dialed another number

and I guess he
had things
going on,
too

none
of this being
what anyone
wanted

or
planned for

hope
in our world
being
a silly thing

most
of the time

but especially

(on that corner
at that bus stop
on that night)

all of it
in us

this
thing
that cannot

be broken

to fit

Incantation

there were plenty of
times I was

thinking of
        (fill in the
                blank)

because you said it was
        what   you
                needed

but really
        (even then)

I knew it was
                nothing more
than

terror
anxiety
self pity
jealousy
meanness
anger
self pity
meanness

and I was happy
to be

involved
    with
        what

was
so
terrible
for
you

and
so
terrible
for
all
the
    others

with
what
was
  so
        unnecessary

as
you
cursed
     at
    your hands

as
you
cursed
the
hours (with your eyes
so closed)

again and again

until

it was   a   magic

spell

(an incantation)

with what we had
never realized was
a ritual

each time we kicked
our dreams further
down the road

with every upturned
laugh and drink at our lips

like a joke being told that
only broken toilets understand

each day starting like this

each day carrying on

the night sky filled
with clouds just
as dark, where we
were as what wanted
to be the moon

standing on
uneven
floors

sitting on
cracked up cement
street corners

with
pins
stuck out
the
backs of our
heads

so sure

the sun
            would
                        never

rise

Tolerant Vacation

inside
  it
     was

(showing)

a   tolerant
         vacation

the second largest
just
   over
       the
           ledge

when you
finally got
away

(for hours)

tiny cup
tiny hotel piss

panda bear tramp stamp
running all over your
ass in the rain

you could've worn clothes

seventeen stitches
down your
        leg

bloody socks
and

tiny   sneakers
on the balcony

no one
          seems

to know what
any of
          this
is
          about

the pieces of
rug

the pieces of
your broken
memory

in this movement
that

keeps

coming
apart

for you

echoing in
the sound
of

what you tell yourself
when you're sure you
don't want any of it
put back together

All Our Love

the card
from Adrianne
and Günter
was a peach
and pink
drugstore
thank you
card

a typed,
canned,
thank you

then
hand written

at the bottom

a
thanking for
the stroller
and my presence
at the party

with their
signatures

and a smiley
face

then
below that

below the
smiley face

written in the same
handwriting:

Lucas,

we heard some
things

from a few
people at
the party

and
we don't want
to offend you

but we just
want to be clear

that
we actually
didn't
name our
son after you

sorry for the
misunderstanding

all our love

then
another smiley
face and

a heart

then some
exes

and
then some ohs

Train

you   crack   the
        sun
big

(bigger than
        a   finger)

           this time

you run the train

    down   again

until   the
        word

midnight   has
      no   meaning

(yes   you've   done
    this
       before)

but   it   goes
         in   a   way

so   that   it
seems

like   the   first
time   is
      always

repeated

                    (again)

you don't believe
  I'm   thinking
    about
            you

(about what's left
    of you and
        how
            harshly
  I say
      things)

it   comes   as
        a
          routine

     in me

two or
   three
      voices

two or
   three
           pictures

  trading
     places

the last one   is the
      bed you   say
you   sleep   in

the real last one
        (though) is

the chair where
    you   sit

        while   you   watch at

what's left of
                the yard

as the road

        across   the
way
            grows
                and

            grows

To My Dear

to my
    dear
        dear
            dear

seeing you
drink

coffeejuice

in the

morning

hair

I've
decided

all
at once

to
live

forever

and

as
one look

I

am

(of course)

inviting

you

(in the matter
            of this self my etc)

to
please
please

come
        with
                me

Her Sex Was Vomit

this
crooked
face

sniffing
for a
smile

this
butterfly
asshole

smell

through a
curved
(wretched)

cunt

in nothing but

rot

(a sickness
of something

long dead)

I should have known

but no, I kept right on going

making fun of people I knew
she hated just so she would
think I was having a good time

Before Sleep

it was what
was in

their eyes

that let you
know

they were not
in the room

anymore

(and were not
 coming back)

a look I practiced
with a mirror

hoping for something
to be passed on

draw it,
one doctor said
handing her a pad and pencil

and all she put
down

were a few squiggles

and said, handing it back,

that's it exactly
      but you won't understand

when she couldn't
tie her shoes

or legally
drive anymore

and soon everything
drained from her face

what color
and light

gone

her name
gone

which kept
me coming back

day after day

looking for
handfuls of
hair left on the floor

and afterwards
before sleep

leaving my shoes
in the yard

so that I could call

all my friends
in the morning
to tell them
    I didn't
       care
         either

In The Morning Before I Left And Then She Left

we had been fooling around
a few weeks when she said
she couldn't do it anymore,

that she was leaving the
country to go back home
to Europe soon and it was
too much

with all the anxiety of leaving,
all that there was to do, the
terror of going back,
of being alone
and having to deal
with me

I just can't do it,

she was saying

I can't

(I please can't)

then she kept postponing
her departure—first by
a week, then three weeks,
then two more weeks,
then an extra month,
then two more weeks on that

all the while I saw almost
nothing of her and got

reports from others who
never really wanted to
talk about it and I was
pretty sure as all this
time was passing by
and she wasn't leaving
that her fear of going was great
but that there was probably
some other guy

someone, I guess, she could
deal with

(better)

then she called me from
out of nowhere

Let's have Indian food
at this Indian place. It's
uptown, she was saying,
Near me, she was saying,

I'm not in Brooklyn anymore,
she was saying,

I'm leaving soon,
she was saying

and we went and ate
and talked and it was nice
and then waiting for a cab
she was telling me I should
come home with her and watch
TV—that she was leaving in
a few days and she couldn't

handle it and there was this
English show she loved about
a boat and all these people

just come and stay a little while

(ah my great and burning
    love of boats)

the room she was subletting
was a wreck—her suitcases
were open with only some
folded clothes and the rest of her
stuff thrown around the floor

there were fifteen foot
floor to ceiling windows and
a raised bed on a semi-loft
near the windows and we
took off our coats and kissed
and crawled into the bed
and she turned on her computer

after we watched five or six
episodes of the program she
showed me pictures of her
home in Europe—what I would
call a chalet style house
though not on a mountain
or in the country
but in a city with lots
of wood beams showing
through the outside white walls
and neighborhood houses
and buildings stacked
up on its sides

she told me about the house
and about her mother and how
her mother calls her all the time
with nothing to say and that
she did not want to go back,
and put her head in her hands
and it seemed like she was crying
but was quiet and I didn't
really know if she was crying
and I didn't say anything

then it was late and I was
sitting on the edge of the
bed with my shoes off and
my feet dangling

and when she came back
from the bathroom with
no bra she put her hands
on my legs and leaned on me
so that her breasts pushed
on me

and we kissed again

(and again)

she said it was too dangerous
outside for me to go now and even
though we both knew that it
wasn't, we, without any coaching,
believed this beautiful lie,
believing all the beautiful lies
that had ever been told,
by us (by everyone)

so that ending up in bed
would somehow not be
anyone's fault

this circumstance
beyond our control

the wave of all the little lies
coming as

warm splinters forced into the
face of truth making it
alright for us to take off
all our clothes and hold
each other

such amazing mouths
we have when they're
not talking

such amazing skin
the way it is electricity
touching tiny hairs

and then
a little sleep

and then it was after sleep
with the sun and the day and
she was only in her black
panties on her hips, and bare feet
pulling back the fifteen foot
blackout curtains, everything
becoming a shattering yellow as she
went down the line opening
shafts of light too bright

to absorb with the eye—her
hair down over her shoulders
her big tits wavering back
and forth as she moved
in front of the many brick buildings
and windows across the way

the whole thing a dance

demanding the city watch
with a spell of bulbous soft curves
moving

as I was in the bed
behind her like
a long dead ghost in
a vaudeville theatre
dressing room, watching while
the magician gets ready
for the main event

showing me in the morning
light all that I missed
while I was alive,

how it is done,

how it can be hidden,

and exactly where it all
comes from

this source of mystery

the source of all the things that
become our lives

from
the center of what
does not have a face

and
produces no sound

yet has a voice

and calls to us

I (too)

in
seeing
what
does
not
reflect
your
face
anymore

in
what
I
tell
myself
is
not
an
end

(people
keep saying
it's ok
to
forgive
me)

I (too)
am
trying
very
much

to
believe
them

Omaha

thank you
      for
         helping
me
  go   insane

the servile day
      to   day
         routine

      I   was
   involved
in   before
   you
        pulled

all   my
         thoughts

apart

    (like pulling a potato
     through a sieve
       in the parking lot
           of   a   dollar store)

was
  too boring

to   go   on
            with

(ah)

being
nuts
though
is
not

as
much
fun
as
the
van gogh paintings
make
      it
          seem

(ah)

but   it
was
a

       joy

to
   watch
your
     anger

and self
   serving
   insecurities

completely

undermine

                        my
                    self
                        esteem

                    and
                    ability
                        to
                            have

rational
            thought

in
    any
    productive
                way

I tell
everyone
at   the
        bus   station

(now)

                about
                        how
            you
                    stabbed
me
        in
            the
        neck

        with

your
     keys

when I
    tried   to

kisss   you

       goodnight

    on   your
        birthday

(you said it   was
    because
       my deodorant smelled
   like
     your
       father)

and   about
  all   the

    blood
       the
        next
          day
  caked
     into
my beard
   and

   my
    clothes

(and Joseph   telling
        me   where   it
             came from
because   I   was   too

                                       drunk to

remember)

I miss
waiting up
for you
without sleep
when you've
        been   gone
                   for
                           three
                           days
or the
way
you   threw
my
     laptop
down the
     stairs
   the   day
after I   got
    it
           because
the   internet
           kept

               going

          out

(so many   other   times

66

I   could go   on about)

now
I take Greyhounds

to random cities

in
        states
                    I've
                        never
wanted to
            go
                to
not
    looking   for
                an
                    answer
but
    for
        something

in

my
    prejudiced
            view
        that

might

    break

        into   me

perhaps with
the same affect

that was the thief
of you

who stole
all   my attention

coming
          home
      with
              three
                  strange
guys

          then cutting

your forearm
with
a steak knife
          when   I
                  protested

the clocks
that stood still

the days missing
all definition
of morning
and
night

smeared on
the windshield
of our broken

and smoldering
used car

out of everything
except gas

only   a hundred and fifty two
miles

to Omaha

Nebraska

I   have
         no
             real

                 idea
what
could
possibly
be
in
Omaha
Nebraska

so
         I   must
       go
            and
                 find
                     out
with
the sun
on all that

corn

maybe
    I'll meet
someone
    with
bulimia

   (a start)

watching her duck out to the bathroom
after she
eats
    only two
       saltine crackers

don't throw up
    I'll say

and
she'll
give
   me
    the
finger

and then
announce

that
   she won't

stop

until

all those green
fields of corn

(in Omaha)

are
        rivers
                of
        pink puke

(flowing, of course,
        from   her   mouth
        to   the   ocean of how beautiful
she   is

(how beautiful
        we
                        all
                                are
in how what we cannot control
        sculpts
                        our days

and
the days of those around us))

you're
        sort
                of   like
        this
                other

        girl
                I

knew

I'll   say

from a different place

I'll say

and she'll keep
giving me   the finger
as she tries
to tie her   hair back
but can't
because she won't
stop giving me
the finger
won't stop
hating
me
and becomes so
frustrated
she starts
to cry

I see this all
happening
at two o'clock
in the afternoon

another thing
you taught me

that crying
happens at
almost any time
of the day or night

there are strange
faces outside
the bus

and a treeless
winter highway
full of snow

I   don't
         know

I just
     thought
   I'd   thank
              you

I   just
     wanted
          to   thank
                      you
in   some   way

most people
I guess
              would not
thank   you
for
              this

perhaps now I'm
starting to understand
why when we went

to meet your parents
you said

please don't be yourself

Riverbend

yellow
of   the

red wet   willow

(going)

this trickle
   of   the   sun

rising out of my hand

                    in wavering lines

as the water bends

to the water wavering way
in what
is

always
always
(   )

   next

Dirtbag Blues

though there
is no water

here
on the sidewalk

and
certainly
no boat

here
on this sidewalk

(all of us
standing in whisky
clusters

or
sitting on the curb
with cigarettes)

the word
shipwrecked

!

! !

(!shipwrecked!)

keeps
going through my mind

A Late One

she can have it

I guess

there's no other

way

when she said she'd be

at my place at ten

and I go searching the parking

lots of bars

for her jeep at two in the

morning

and there is no

sign she was ever here

and I buy a drink and drink

half not having anything to say

this space

of what is so wild

and uncontrolled

taking from us what

cannot be won back

another night

that tells me

something about

my past I did not listen to

and am not listening to now

as I hum a melody that says

all things missing or

not understood

can be found

knowing it is a lie

not wearing a jacket

when I need a jacket

cold hands

and the cold plumes of my

breath burning my

lungs and the inside of my mouth

as I walk

when I get   home

I have left all the

lights on

and I have left the

door unlocked and open slightly

(incase she

showed up while I was out)

as I lay down on

the top of the bed

in my clothes

and do not

sleep for many hours

with what mysteries there

are plainly unsolved

my dirty shoes on

the sheets

a cut on my forehead that

will not heal

this way of knowing

that

everything ends but nothing

ever stops

Just To See

just to see

anyway

what it would

be like

the face

stretched over

timebones

to

a laugh

with what is curious

where the roots go through the dirt

like gears meshed in a clock

finally bigger than death

They Find The White

they find the white
in the
death of a thing

(if they are lucky)

and then there are lines drawn
through a ritual ring in the sand

wordless and with a
sense of fraud brought
on by a meaningless fear

you say sometimes

I will smash skulls
against what is enormous

against the monstrous
defeat

drinking blood

spitting blood

breathing blood

you know
(sometimes)

this is true

though you

know

there is
a place

of
places

to
the side

of what
is understood

the quiet of where
you have not been

that squeezes
the throat

Opera

they were singing opera
and putting on a show
with some costumes
and a harmonica—
the dirtbag aria—
which, even soaked
in gin with dead bugs
is about love, about the
end of what should
have gone on forever—
even though nothing
goes on forever (but it
should have this time, goddamn it!)
we'll get it back, they're
singing—the harmonica
squealing along—and
outside the world
has wiped its ass with
the sky—a beautiful
smattering of stars
in deep blue bringing on
what all the sullied mouths
standing open are calling
the terror of night—we'll get
it back—with crooked fingers,
with crooked hearts now for sure
—we'll get it back—the songs will
not stop—they rise and grow and now
sound more like screaming—the shriek
of the human voice, unmatched by any
other animal in the wilderness—the audience
is trying to figure out if it's pain
or joy—they're trying to figure
out what they're supposed to feel

Tonight

the moon looks like
shit tonight

but that's okay
there's some spaghetti
and sauce that I've
been waiting all day
to eat,

and tomorrow there's
a new dark roast
at
the coffee house

the street is finally
quiet

and I've decided
this is good, too

the moon looks like
shit tonight

but last week I didn't
throw up when Regina
had her birthday party
and I was too drunk
to walk home

my pants, knees, shredded
the morning
on the sidewalk
burning my eyes

some traffic is now going
over the drawbridge in the
distance—the yellow
lights coming in from
the west, the red lights
heading east

a stranger version of
the cosmos

a manmade milky way
racing to get out of town

the moon still looks
like shit tonight

and the falling
little leaves
have all blown
into the gutter

not with a cherry blossom
wind but with
chainsaws and backhoes

to start the new housing
development behind
my apartment

mudholes and puddles
of brown water and waste

the moon looks like
shit tonight

but maybe an eye, a
pair of eyes, will
move into one of the
new houses and with long
lashes, see me, as the
person I'd always
thought I'd become

you'll get there
the eyes will say

I'll come with you

and the eyes will have
a five year old
who only talks
to the homeless
and a dog they can't feed

so I'll get texts
that read:
come on over
and oh, can you
pick up some
dog food on the
way

even though there is
no place that sells
dog food between
the beautiful eyes
and my place

of course,
I'll say

then later
the eyes will tell
me how they don't really
drink anymore
as they open their
second bottle of
wine for us

and everyone
in the room understands
the elasticity of
the truth in supporting
all our ways in becoming
something we are not

and I will help the
eyes move a
used futon across
the apartment
so we can sit, all three
of us, crammed all
together near an
open window

for when we can look up
without so much pain
in our necks and in our
backs

and the night is released
from its metaphor of terror

and the dark of it acts as a
pillow for thought

a jailbreak from what we

were robbed of only
a few hours before
in the daylight

and the shitty moon
is the best it's ever been

rising like a white whale
over the hills

to swallow the hills
in its white light

devouring us and the apartment
and the futon

leaving what is left of our
hearts and dreams in the
soft glow of what finally needs nothing

It's In Her Voice

it's in her voice

now
in the way it cracks

how she's going to be
when she's an old woman

too focused on her knees

too frustrated to get what
she wants
              (or simply never had)

how simple
her anger will be

how easily it will
break her rotting
teeth

(the flaking bits)

falling from her mouth

the sound

covering finally
the last lightness
that is there

from when she was
young

and always wore a hat

this heart tone that warms
when she asks a question
and is genuinely

not embarrassed

and you can hear how big

her eyes used to be
in wanting to know things

how big everything
used to be

before it had a name

Married

there's this guy in
the neighborhood
who got an air
conditioner
from me

the air conditioner
was meant for
someone else

I had stolen
it from work

then because of
some electrical
issue at the place
it was supposed
to go to

he
ended
up with it

I found out about
all this weeks
after it happened

anyway, he had
the air conditioner

and he knew
(I) somehow

it   (got
came   it
from   to
me   him)

so he always
stopped
to chat

in what was
his way of
saying thanks

this man
whose name
I could never
remember
Chad
Chet
Brad
something

stops me
after I'm leaving
the bar

on my way
home

on my way
to piss

hey!
how ya doing?!
wow!
thanks again for the a.c.!

excited

he is always excited
or completely exhausted

only these two feelings

only these two feelings
for so many

going with my
old lady to wait
for the bus,
he says

trying to get
to work,
he says

it's very late and
this he isn't so
excited about

he tells me
how he does
security and some
barbacking at a
place across town

interesting,
I say

we been married
thirty four years,
he says

and I'm forty seven!
he yells

she's standing way
down the street
alone
on the corner by the curb

a small round woman
looking at her feet
looking at the sky
looking at her feet again

I'm trying to retire,
he says

the whole thing you
see,
he says

was that I got
married in Brazil
when I was eleven,

he kind of laughs
he kind of shrugs,

she was supposed
to be my sister,

and he makes a
motion toward her
over his shoulder,

but my daddy killed

her daddy right here
on canal street back
in the seventies

so we ended up
being married

she's from Brazil

so we got married
in Brazil

interesting,
I say

yeah,
he says

and I'm leaning
on one leg
in a way to
tell him I must
be going

that I must be
going now

yeah,
he says again

then says,
well I won't keep you,

ok,
I say

thanks again for
the a.c.,
he says

it's saving Pepe's life!

I don't know who
Pepe is

if Pepe is their child
or their dog

none of what he says
makes much sense to me

it's a short interaction
and I think maybe
I should say
something to encourage
him

but I don't

he shakes my hand

and walks off to
his ancient lonely curb-standing
bride from Brazil

the sidewalk continues

I only get three more blocks
before I have to stop
and piss between
two houses

ducking down a
sort of driveway
sort of alley

I am not so excited
about this

and the lies I tell myself
have the eyes
of the entire neighborhood
on me

as I am ready to break into
a run at any slight movement or sound

I am filled with so
many hopes

most about
piss being easy

some about

there
being
music

and
that
just for now

there will be

no
lights
at all

in the world
that will find me

until the pissing
is done

(then of course)

when the pissing
is done

and I have
pulled up my pants
and am ready to go

I will stand on my toes

and call and whistle

for everyone
of them

the dim ones
the dull ones
the ones so
bright they have
their own knives and hearts

to please

hunt for me

all night

in every shadow
I have ever passed

The Piece

the piece that
was left

with a cracked
edge

the only thing
I hadn't stolen

the only thing
I hadn't told
all the others was mine

in the worn slots of
another's world
view

this blue

now cloudlessness

in the talk we
will have

when my friend
gets back

the things we
will say about
the dead

the
magic words

we will use

in the stories
we tell

that let us go on longer
than the dead

Now After

when it comes
there now
in the

(one)
    crash crash

to burn
merry

(burn
white)

this island
smile

floats

from our
smiling fists

to build
hello
there

flower

hello
there
again

sunflower

Song

there's a song
I sing that
no one knows

that pushes
the blood out
of my eyes
like tears

no, no, I'm
not crying

this is something
else entirely

a melody of red
running down
a mountain
in relief

there's a song
I sing that has
many words

that I always
forget and must
whistle as though
the words were
meant to sound
like a dented
flute

as though this

noise is a language
understood by
the chosen

or perhaps ghosts
by an open door

there's a song
I sing that fails
in how yellow
the sky needs
to be

and though I
don't understand this
I have been taught
that failure is success

a modern day
interpretation

that many days
I need to be true

there's a song
I sing that
won't let me
out, promising
a future paved
in endless praise

there's a song
I sing whose
bones are gray

standing as a reminder

of what was

and what will come

at times

(many times)

this song I
sing goes
on and on
and will not die

as friends
and strangers

watch me
with that look
that wishes
they had the
courage to
tell me to
shut the fuck up

this song
I sing that
tells me it's
very old

though I invent
new lines all the time
and know in truth it
can be a liar

the song sails along

blood bones and all

telling me
the hand it holds

is real

with lines
and harmonies

sometimes with too much weight
sometimes being torn away

many times
rising

from where
it is best to
leave things be

the air of my lungs
coming in

and
passing from the edge
of one ear to another
what sings
with light

that shines
so many times
without a sound

Stars

our
   too
      much

  fuck   you
        (face)

(turning on
its back)

in
a
(slow)
breath

pin
prick
lights

run
out
over
gutter
lips

(last four dollars)

hanging
from above

hair
brown
brown

shit

eyes
up

shit
shit
street

Last Summer

on the water

with only noses up
to touch the sky

and our lungs full of mud
and stink

in the reeds bending breeze
as our breathing turned to blood

you kept telling me the leaves
had no trees

these bare lines
against a blue home

and I wanted to say no

it was the other way around

that you were wrong

this place with the branches blowing

(our thoughts so terribly in us)

and your hair sprawled out and
floating on the surface like
a lotus lily wrapped around the white of your face

The One Goes By

the one goes by

a blue
dream

not much
to talk
about

until
then there
is
the
thing
with weight

as two

it drifts
it falls

and
anticipates
a lightness

that can
wish for
a floating
without cause

the way it thinks
it was always
supposed to be

after that
they call

it three

and it comes
like a freight train

heavy
and
with
purpose

an
unyielding
movement
on
a track
into the distance

a
metallic
river
burning
through
a mountain

the whistle
blast

and what
stands
idle
must flee

(this) to
what falls
(in front)

the other
side though

where you
can count
easily on your
fingers

a solace

we have
not yet
seen

as our
children
fill
rooms
and buildings
with drawings
of it

assuring
us
it
is alive

with their
lines and color

with their
songs

with how
they do not
blink

in the activity
of terror

in the activity
of our pretending
a way around terror

A Note

yes

I
can
also love

you
later

(I guess)

when
I
have
back

at least
some
of
the
things

(after
you're
gone)

lost
(stolen)

I
guess

(I guess)

it's
just
easier
for
me

that
way

A Footstep To The Largeness

you're listening to the
bugs of the yard

and you keep
thinking you've missed
something

mostly it is a settling
and an easing

but they'll
be back out to the porch

and then the noise of want
will begin again

you are thinking there
is a piece

you think of
the space that is

the distance between
the ends of no's and
yeses

where sometimes
they can mean
the same thing

and with the street
in front of you

this hole

without
an edge

without
a center

where
you want
to get up

and without any real
understanding

walk it

(and maybe
then you will
know)

having at least
tried

to get across

what is unseen

to what has
swallowed
what is unseen

with ice
and the crush
of ice

to climb
this mountain

that fits
in the palm of your hand

Sometimes Always

sometimes
always
sometimes

more than
sometimes

we are
bigger
       bigger
             smash

in the
morning

on the edges of
our parts

in the evening when
we are filled with
what we could never
have conceived

when loss
is such a grace

(which

    (I suppose)

makes

laughter

ho ha ha

(as it   happens)

such
a miracle)

            !

(!)

Out Here

when Jason
was giving me
a ride home
he said
the local
government
keeps the streets
out here
all broken up
to stop the
drunks from
speeding

his old Pontiac
rocking and
hitting each
hole
without
him making
a move to
miss them

or flinching

fuck 'em,
he said

slam
shake
shake

the whole
thing is

stupid,
he said

(slam)
shake

then he was
telling me
about all
the cocaine
he had sold
in Alabama

all he money
he had made
and lost

other cars he
owned that
weren't around
anymore

(like new friends
who'd slunk off
when his luck ran out
and his back was turned
and found somewhere
else to be)

(mobile?)
shake
shake

the fortune of
lawyers paid and
gone with no

time served

and there was this
stripper I was seeing

long black straight hair

I did her in the ass
at the W Hotel

right by the pool

she was a mess
I hope she's alright

she's gone now
too

slam
shake

he had been at
the restaurant
three months

the way he held
his knife in
his fist while
cutting onions

the way he moved
through us from the
grill to the prep station
to the walk-in

like watching a

lion walk around
the pen of a petting zoo

another slam
another shake

the warm
night air
going through
the windows

All of Your Poems

all of your poems
are about dog
shit,

she says,

why don't you write
about something
else,

she says,

no one wants
to read about
dogs
shiting,

she says

she thinks there
is something wrong
with me

she immediately disagrees
with everything I say

she does this because
she feels she is standing
up for herself

(it's funny because she
does it the most when
she is in a good mood

an extension of
her feeling confident)

when we pull
up to the gate
of the state park
the girl who is
watching
the guardhouse
is standing outside
smoking

she is a good looking
girl with long brown
straight hair

and she does not care
really
that we are pulling up

nice,
I say and laugh

she takes what I say
and my laugher
for sarcasm and says,
why can't she smoke
she probably needs
a break

christ, I say,
why do you
always do this, I say

all right, she says, calm down

she says, what's wrong with you

if only she had
an idea

(if only I had
      an idea)

at the top of the hill
by the end of the parking
lot the lake begins

we stand there looking
at it,

looking at the rock face from
the mountain that comes
down to meet the
water

glassy

serene

it's beautiful,
she says

thank you for
the narration,
I say

we do not look at each
other but I
know she wants to
hate me with her eyes

with her whole face

in a way that I would
understand the purity
of her anger

and how I deserve it

but there's only so much
you can throw at each other
in a parking lot by a lake

and she wants a nice day

and I want a nice day

everyone always wants a nice day

perhaps for her birthday I'll suggest
a fight

a planned fight where we scream
our lungs out about forgotten dinners
and misplaced hugs

so the rest of the year may be a nice day

we start out of the lot to
the edge of the dirt and grass
and there are trees and the
puzzled patterns of the leaves
and the trees and the sun
on the ground

the water makes a certain
noise though I don't know

how a lake that doesn't
move can make a noise

when we turn up the path
to head
to castle point

there is a couple
standing on the side
with a brown black german shephard

squatted on its haunches

taking
a shit

a breeze blowing

a coolness off the water

she pauses a half step
and grunts

but it isn't until we
are past them

when we are some
paces away out
of ear shot
that she says,

don't say a fucking
word,

still without
looking at me,

not one fucking word,

walking fast ahead

leaving me behind

I could feel my notebook
in my pocket

as I watch her go

if only what made sense
didn't present itself
so simply sometimes

the obviousness of the trick
of the truth fools everyone

even the
most intelligent

and it's only after it comes out
of us

trying to make
a melody

so that someone
else may hear

and know

what goes
on inside

that it starts

(layered,
walled, fogged)

this muffled song
translated again
through the
small eyes of
what sees so
little

and then of
course

comes the invention
of how we must
behave

    (a costume of
    smiles

    for a mouthful
    of laughter)

and
just being an asshole

isn't
much of an excuse

(not lately anyway)

Gasping Again

he was gasping again
but no one moved
this time

no one called out
for a nurse

or went to get
anyone

we'd been waiting
on this for
days
          (months)
etc

all of us now
without words

and how
without words
he wouldn't
let go

and even
if there were
instructions

he probably
wouldn't listen

propping himself
up with his

cataract milk eyes

as none of us
help

he then
making some
sounds that maybe
may have been words

gasping and wheezing
now with phlegm

like
someone pulling
on the chord
of a lawnmower
that won't start

like this
the whole way

for all the minutes
in front of us

what we knew

what we've always
known

unable to
look at him

unable to look
at each other anymore

our little hands

squeezing our tiny fingers

our fucking feet in comfortable
fucking shoes standing on the
freshly mopped linoleum

It Holds This Going From Across The Hall

the way he's angry
without cause
when she puts on
a new pair of pants,
as he shakes his pack
of cigarettes to feel
how many are left—
a pigeon wing cut from
the still bleeding bird—
a falling whistle
trying to keep the tune—
they share an orange
while a bee bangs on
the glass of the window
on the door—there's a
bit of sleep in there
too—guitar strings
hold up her last
marionette thoughts of
the day when her heart
was beating through
her breasts as a small raccoon
waiting for night—a furry
thief he'll shoo from
the trash

The Poems Without Fuck

she told me to
write pretty ones

ones people
will like

(people other
than just you,
she said)

and then things
will happen

"They don't have to
be about flowers,"
she said,
"but maybe not
so many with
the word fuck."

I won't say what
I was staring at

"Some people
like fuck,"
I said.

"Yes,"
she said,
"but not at
breakfast. Poetry
is all about
breakfast."

none of what
she was saying
was making much
sense to me

"Poetry is a big
bite of a scrumptious
meal that starts things
going,"
she said.

"I don't know if
that's exactly true,"
I said.

now I wasn't
staring at anything

"Well, of course
it's not true,"
she said.
"Nothing's, true,"
she said.

I was leaning on
the table, propping
my head in my hand,
tired

"I don't know
if that's exactly
true," I said.

she smiled
and said my name

I was going to say
her name back to her
maybe sing it like a song

but did not say anything

then she started
going on about
a dream she had

there wasn't much
left to drink and
probably nothing
was open

I was with
her voice

in a room that was
not any room I was
familiar with

I thought about
writing a poem called
The Never Ending Nightmare Dream

every dream when described
by another person sounds the same,

a list of inane events
of people and things
that have little or no meaning
to you

or even, really, the dreamer

a random bag
of broken groceries

bought while high at
two in the morning from

the bare shelves of
a gas station that should have
been closed years
ago

then I thought,
no,
The Never Ending Nightmare Dream Of Fuck

I giggled

I giggled and knew

how this poem,
though I would write it,
would never see the
light of day

and about how in
writing it down would
jumble the whole thing,
making it go one direction
then another, off a cliff,
climb back up the cliff

the way thinking
and translating thinking
goes

such a
heartbreaking beauty
in my head

(even with the giggle)

it would never be
right

when brought into
the world

like
the way
she was looking at
her hand holding
the glass she was holding

with what was
right then
the type of tenderness

she had always
wanted to have

for others

140

Such A Sunday Night

she is screaming,
        get the fuck out

it started low like a talking
    with
    her voice
   coming only slightly through
the wall

but by the third
        time   she
       said it   she yelled it

and you knew something was
       wrong

get the fuck out—at the
          top of her lungs

then over and
       over until it almost had no meaning

now he is
   saying things
(in a low talking)

I turn off the computer

when they first got together
I wondered how
         or
              why
but I guess I do that

with all
     people

she was friendly and matter
        of fact

he always wore some kind of hat
     and had this twisted look on his face
never saying
    a   word

if you met them in the
   street he would nod
and then stand there doing
nothing with that face
until she stopped talking and it was time to go

it's been two years and I
   found out his name
     last month
when going through their
mail

they used to live
         downstairs
now they live
     upstairs
     next
       to me

she graduated college
     and started her
   own non-for-profit

and in the fall is going
to London on a Fulbright

Scholarship

he, I think, is some sort
                    of cook

it was remarkable how someone
so pretty and smart could remain by herself
in that apartment for so
        long

            then he showed up

she used to get drunk and
demand I give her
    my copy of Basquiat's
        biography
saying how
    she loved his
work, talking about
how she made her own
                clothes and loved
                the fashion
                and art
                of
                the '80's

you have to seriously get the fuck out

        Fuck you! —he screams

they always seemed pleasant enough
                        together

I'll call the cops! Get the fuck out
                    or I'll call
                        the fucking cops!

143

Call the fucking cops, I don't care!
                    I pay rent here!

now my ear is pressed against
    the wall and everything is
        very clear

            a door slams
her feet go down the hall
heavy and shaking the
            ceiling

it's quiet

then she comes back
and says
        plainly

you have got to leave
you have got to leave
seriously, you have got to leave

he says something I cannot hear

then
she:
get the fuck out!

then he is screaming fuck
then she is screaming fuck

the screaming goes up and down
                    then up
                    then down

then the front door slams
   and he is   gone

                                (there is a moment)
a beat of quiet

then there are her feet

going in the hall again
but not as heavy now

another moment

something has settled

then she is talking

plainly

she paces across the floor
all the way down, all the way back
talking

having called someone

(not the cops)

her voice goes faster as she moves

the word hospital is used
      a few times

I am planted in the middle of the apartment and
she is moving past me then past
   me again as she
   paces the whole length so I cannot hear

all of what she says

what I put together is this:

she was at the hospital
    getting staples
        in her head

it was late
and he left work to meet her
at the emergency room
but did not ask her
how she was when he got there
or offer any type of encouragement
or kind words
and was in fact falling asleep
as the procedure was going on

she got mad and told
him if he was so tired
to go home
he gave no
resistance and left

when she got home
after getting the staples
in her head

(why she needed the staples
I never found out)

he was still mostly apathetic
and still mostly falling asleep

it started with a serious talk
and then she went berserk

berserk being a word
that comes from
   old German, from the term
bear shirt—a certain type of
man would put on a shirt made
from a bear skin and work
himself into an uncontrolled
frenzy for battle
        there was no stopping these bear shirts,
        either all of you were dead
        or all of them were dead
   they were greatly feared
        (probably even by each other)

she cries now

it is terrible to hear
    and I feel stupid
    for listening
    and the weight of her
    sorrow makes me
    feel alone

there's a voice coming from
        the phone
            that can
    do nothing for her

I can do nothing for her

the anguish so complete
    she can do nothing
        for
            herself

in this flood
drowning any sense
of connection and repair

a sun lit light that won't shut off
illuminating suddenly all the
idiotic things he's ever done
with a shadow over anything
ever nice as a mask for his
true motives and stupidities

she's telling the voice again and again
   what happened, what he said—he said, Fuck
you!
   and she shouts it like he shouted it—Fuck you!
he said Fuck you! he said Fuck you!

and all the while the tension in
the tone of her throat saying again and again

                how could I have been
                    so wrong?

I start thinking that there is no possible
way they will get back together

but then I remember so much that
had been lost

that was not found

but remade

built on a ground that
had already been flattened

words and time

or a lack of words and a simple
healing in how we as creatures
are forgetful creatures

and this couple will eat granola
in the morning again

saying silly bunny button things
to each other while listening to NPR

but I also wonder about looking
someone in the eye after such
a Sunday night

of what comes back
after you've forgotten

when it rises without
warning

the roar

the crashing of
the noise coming
over the top inside

that you cut off

then nothing

a chirp

I turn the computer back on
a documentary about

the plague

I hear her voice for a while
then I don't hear her voice

then the documentary is over
and I go to bed in the dark
and there is no sound at all
anymore

in my mind I think about
what she will be like
tomorrow, sitting at
her desk, at her non-for-profit
with a cup of coffee she does not really drink
as people keep asking her what's wrong

and she will say something about
the staples in her head and the
doctors and the nurses,
without any real answer as to why
her mouth will not stop being so crooked

biting down
on confusions and anger

that have always been there
but somehow now seem new

somehow with all that has gone on
a surprise

tonight in telling
someone you love to get out and go
fuck themselves

no matter how many
times it happens
it is always new

is always
a surprise

to hear it
to say it

Another Day Amusing Myself

another day
amusing myself

slowed
arms

standing

with boxes

making

(the radio)

the space I need getting bigger
and bigger

to break
even

knowing now
my childish
ways have
no more modes or models

(a cut wing
feather
falling)

and like
that

something

has landed

new

in
a memory
I did not
understand
was a memory

(poof)

the joy of
what comes down
but will not stay

in
each hour

it seems

there is this long
walk from the
place of my feet

that I am told
leads

home

About the Author

Born and raised in Upstate New York, Christopher Heffernan's poetry and fiction have appeared in magazines and journals all over the country such as *The Writer's Journal, Pacific Coast Journal, Sierra Nevada Review, Whisky Island, Big Muddy, 34th Parallel, Louisiana Literature* and *The Madison Review.* He is the author of another book of poetry titled *Rag Water* and spends much of his time working and walking in the sun.

Fomite

Writing a review on social media sites for readers will help the progress of independent publishing. To submit a review, go to the book page on any of the sites and follow the links for reviews. Books from independent presses rely on reader-to-reader communications.

For more information or to order any of our books, visit:
http://www.fomitepress.com/our-books.html

More poetry from Fomite...

Anna Blackmer — *Hexagrams*
L. Brown — *Loopholes*
Sue D. Burton — *Little Steel*
Christine Butterworth-McDermott — *Evelyn As*
Christine Butterworth-McDermott — *The Spellbook of Fruit and Flowers*
David Cavanagh— *Cycling in Plato's Cave*
Rajnesh Chakrapani — *The Repetition of Exceptional Weeks*
James Connolly — *Picking Up the Bodies*
Benjamin Dangl — *A World Where Many Worlds Fit*
Greg Delanty — *Behold the Garden*
Greg Delanty — *Loosestrife*
Mason Drukman — *Drawing on Life*
J. C. Ellefson — *Foreign Tales of Exemplum and Woe*
Anna Faktorovich — *Improvisational Arguments*
Barry Goldensohn — *Snake in the Spine, Wolf in the Heart*
Barry Goldensohn — *The Hundred Yard Dash Man*
Barry Goldensohn — *The Listener Aspires to the Condition of Music*
Barry Goldensohn — *Visitors Entrance*
R. L. Green — *When You Remember Deir Yassin*
KJ Hannah Greenberg — *Beast There—Don't That*
Kevin Hadduck — *Beloved Brother*
John Hawkins — *Mirror to Mirror*
Christopher Heffernan — *[laughter]*
Gail Holst-Warhaft — *Lucky Country*
Judith Kerman — *Definitions*
Yahia Lababidi — *Quarantine Notes*
Joseph Lamport — *Enlightenment*
Raymond Luczak — *A Babble of Objects*
Kate Magill — *Roadworthy Creature, Roadworthy Craft*
Tony Magistrale — *Entanglements*
Gary Mesick — *General Discharge*

Fomite

Fomite

Made in the USA
Middletown, DE
10 September 2023

37822200R00102